AF230625

The Life
of
The Black Panther
of
Wewoka, Oklahoma
As Told By
Mr. Bernie Patel
and His
11th Grade
History Class

Written By
Sharon Kaye Hunt

The Life of the Black Panther of Wewoka, Oklahoma

Copyright © 2021 by Sharon Kaye Hunt

All rights reserved. No part of this publication may be reproduced, distributed, or transmitted in any form or by any means, including photocopying, recording, or other electronic or mechanical methods, without the prior written permission of the author, except in the case of brief quotations embodied in critical reviews and certain other non-commercial uses permitted by copyright law.

ISBN
978-1-954932-32-6 (Paperback)
978-1-954932-31-9 (eBook)

Contents

Acknowledgements

I thank Mr. Steve Hawkins and Mr. Charles Tauhlbert, Oklahoma Librarians. Without the assistance of the Hunt Brothers and Mr. Henry and Ruddy Brown, my research would not be complete.

Thanks to Mr. James Coody Johnson for Johnson Grove Grade School.

Introduction

Mr. Bernie Patel, an eleventh grade history teacher, assigned his class of twenty students a research project on lawyer James Coody Johnson, known as 'The Black Panther'.

He was an outstanding African-American who had made major contributions to the town of Wewoka, the state of Oklahoma and the nation as a whole in the early nineteenth hundreds.

Mr. Bernie Patel

(Students I will now hear your research reports on James Coody Johnson. As I call your name, please give me the title and the main points of your research report.)

Mr. Bernie Patel, B.S. M.A.
11th Grade History Teacher

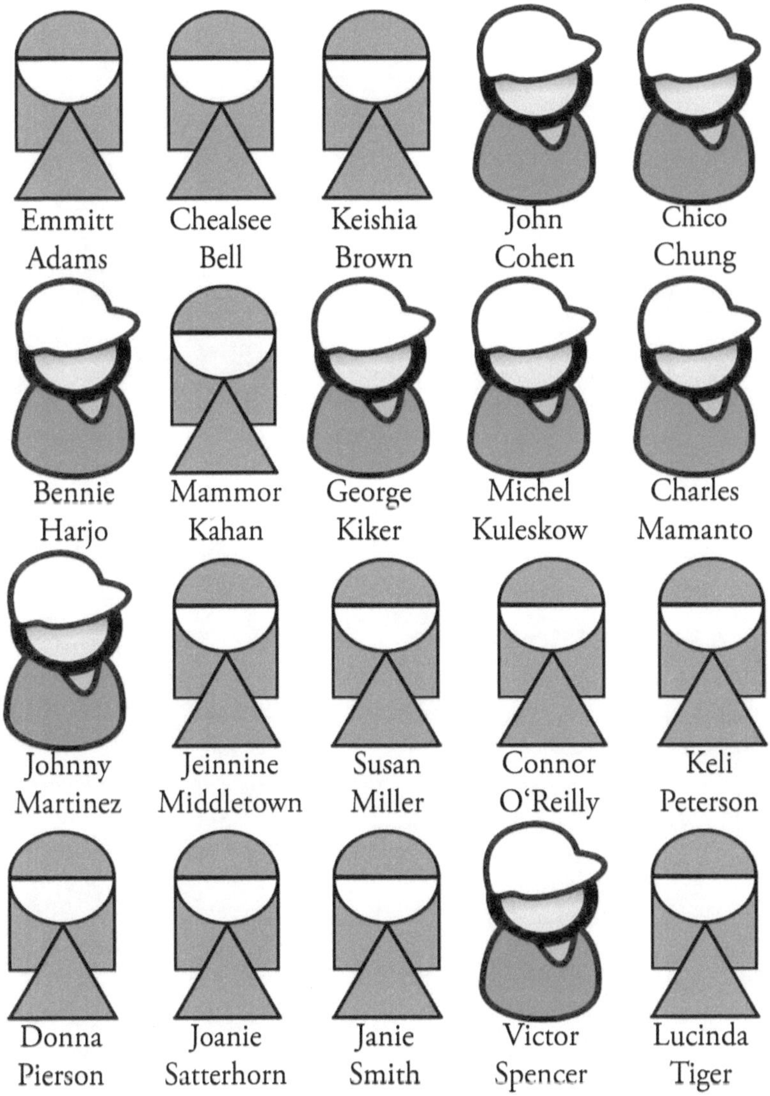

Emmitt Adams	Chealsee Bell	Keishia Brown	John Cohen	Chico Chung
Bennie Harjo	Mammor Kahan	George Kiker	Michel Kuleskow	Charles Mamanto
Johnny Martinez	Jeinnine Middletown	Susan Miller	Connor O'Reilly	Keli Peterson
Donna Pierson	Joanie Satterhorn	Janie Smith	Victor Spencer	Lucinda Tiger

11th Grade History Class

Birth

His father was a slave named Robert Johnson.

James Coody Johnson was born on July 27, 1864 one year before the end of the Civil War in 1865.

He was born in Ft. Gibson, Okla.

His mother's name was Elizabeth Davis Johnson.

His Father was the African Creek interpreter for the Seminole nation.

He was born a Creek Freedmen.

His mother was protected as a refugee during the Civil War.

Emmitt
Adams

Early Childhood

Reared in Wewoka, Oklahoma.

His mother was a refugee before his birth during the Civil War.

He worked with his dad and stayed on a farm.

Chealsea
Bell

Presbyterian Mission School

James Coody Johnson preferred to sign his name J. Coody Johnson.

He attended a religious school.

Students were African-Americans, Creek and Seminole Indians.

School was located north of Wewoka.

Keishia
Brown

Higher Education

He graduate college from Lincoln University.

J. Coody Johnson went to school on an American Indian Scholarship.

He returned to Wewoka after graduating from college.

Lincoln University is located in Chester, Pennsylvania.

Chico
Chung

Cowboy on the Range

James Coody Johnson loved to ride horses in Oklahoma and the West.

Rode horses in Indian Territory in 1884.

He was an employee with a cattle company.

He rode as a cowboy on the range with other black cowboys in Mexico, Arizona and Texas.

He was a cowboy for ten and a half years.

John
Cohen

Indian Interpreter

J. Coody Johnson was bilingual.

He served as a Creek Indian Interpreter.

He served as an interpreter for a judge whose name was Isaac Parker.

He spoke Creek and Seminole languages.

Benny
Harjo

Practicing Law in Wewoka

He passed the bar exam to practice law.

He studied law under Judge Isaac Parker.

He did not attend Law School.

He first practiced law on Cedar Street.

He was admitted to practice in the federal courts.

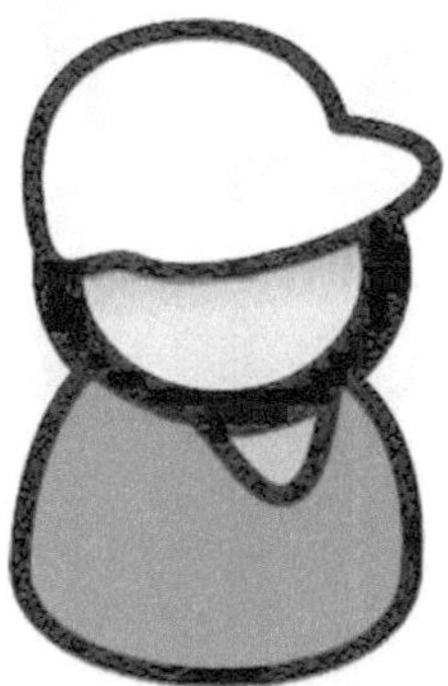

Mammar
Kahan

Creek Indian Politics

Johnson was a high Creek political figure.

J. Coody could speak Creek and Seminole language.

He served as an advisor to Seminole Chief Halputta Micco.

George
Kiker

Member of the Warriors

He was a leading Creek politician.

James Coody Johnson served more than two terms in the Creek House of Warriors.

The Creek Indians sent J. Coody Johnson of special delegations to Washington, DC representing them during allotment period.

His grandfather was a slave to a Coweta Chief of the Creek nation— William McIntosh.

He served as secretary of the Creek Nation.

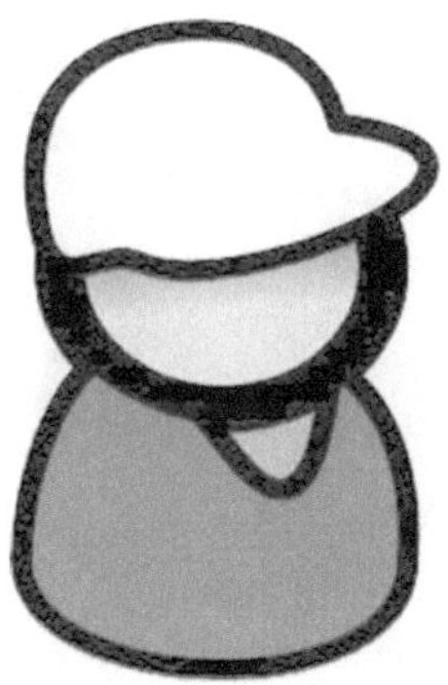

Micheal
Kuleskow

Representatives of the Seminole Nation

He was the main interpreter for the Seminole Indian Nation.

He had citizenship in the Seminole Nation.

He assisted in getting Seminole Indian allotments.

He served as a private secretary to the main chief of the Seminole Nation.

Charles
Mamanto

Independent Fair Owner

He held two fairs for African American children.

He was once the president of the Negro State Fair Association.

The Negro State Fair was held in Wewoka in 1919.

It was said that Wiley Post appeared at J. Coody Johnson's Ranch at a Negro State Fair in 1920.

He assisted in putting on Oklahoma's first Negro Independent State Fair.

The first Negro Fair was held in 1915 at Muskogee.

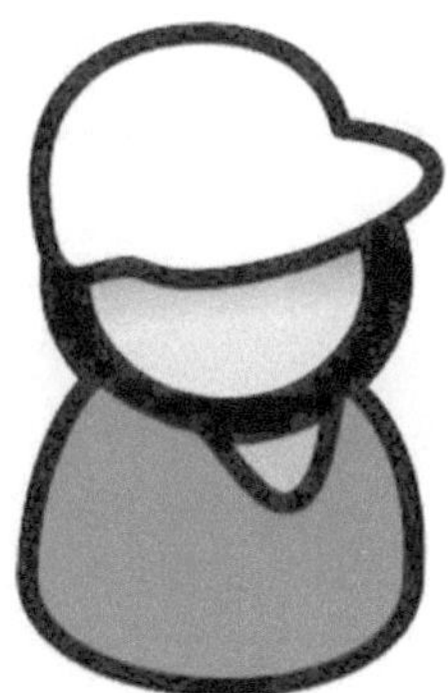

Johnny
Martinez

The Black Panther

J. Coody Johnson was named the Black Panther by the Creek Indians.

He was an African-American Creek lawyer.

Susan
Miller

James Coody Johnson

Independent Oilman

He had oil leases.

The name of his oil company was Black Panther Oil and Gas Company.

Johnson was oil entrepreneur.

Jeannine
Middleton

Negro Protection League

He formed his own Negro Protection League.

Johnson fought against "Jim Crow" laws.

Johnson served as lawyer to protect African-Americans rights to full citizenship in Oklahoma in 1907.

Compared to Fredrick Douglas, Booker T. Washington and Martin Luther King, Jr..

He testified before the U.S. Supreme Court.

Conner O'
Reilly

Location of Law Office Building

Name of law office Johnson, J. Coody Building Building built in 1916.

Location of Office Building 124 North Wewoka Street Wewoka, Oklahoma.

Building listed in the National Register Black Industry Building

Name of Architect/Builder/Engineer: Witherspoon & Woods

First Law office 1907

Period of significance: 1900-1924 1925-1949.

The Johnson Building on the corner of Wewoka Avenue and Cedar Street 124 N. Wewoka.

Building listed in the National Register NR 8500174.

Only black building in the 20th century black-owned establishment on Wewoka's Main Street.

Keli
Peterson

Landowner and Location of Home

James Coody Johnson lived five miles north of Wewoka, Oklahoma.

He owned many acres of land and mineral rights.

He owned the Black Panther Hotel in Wewoka.

He owned two hotels in Wewoka.

His plantation or ranch was located five miles north of Wewoka.

Donna
Pierson

Organized Land Allotments

Attorney Johnson served as representative for Seminole and Creek Indian families oil and land allotments.

He organized land allotments for Creek and Seminole freedmen.

Joanie
Satterhorn

African-American Advocate

Attorney Johnson assisted freedmen to get land in Oklahoma.

He fought for marriage freedom for African-Americans.

He prevented Oklahoma from becoming a "Jim Crow" State.

He served two terms as Grand Master of the Colored Masons of Oklahoma.

Janie
Smith

Johnson Grove Elementary School

Attorney Johnson established the elementary school for African-American children.

North of Wewoka Highway (Hwy) 9.

The school was a country school for "Negro boys and girls"—Children— grades 1-8.

Johnson Grove school was part of the J. Coody Johnson estate 1927.

Seminole County Wewoka, Okla 74884.

First school was located on the Johnson Ranch 1927-1964.

Johnson Grove closed due to integration in the late 60's.

Final Alumni Last Names

-Benjamins-Moores

-Browns-Obys

-Bruners-O'quinns

-Coates

-Coopers

-Doolittles-Perrys

-Frees-Ponders

-Hunts-Thomas

-Kemps-Terrell

-Madkins-Zollicoffey

Present Location

-5 miles north of Wewoka on Highway 56 turn left at four way stop light and turn left of Hwy 2 miles west on Hwy 9 formerly a Redbrick three room school house.

-Currently a Redbrick private home.

Victoria
Spencer

Burial Grounds

Attorney James Coody Johnson is buried in the Johnson Cemetery near Wewoka, Oklahoma.

He died February 1927.

He is buried in a cemetery north of Wewoka.

His mother, father and daughter are buried near Coody Johnson.

His monument has the date 1864-1927.

His wishes were to be buried near his relatives.

Lucinda
Tiger

Mr. Patel
Rap-up

Article I

We Stand

For the right of the voice of men to be heard in their own Government.

For Democracy that is an actuality—not ritualistic.

COODY JOHNSON CROSSES GREAT DIVIDE

THE LATE J. COODY JOHNSON

Prominent Creek Freedman who died suddenly Sunday at his home, Wewoka. Story of funeral on editorial page.

**Picturesque
Creek Freedman Buried Tuesday**

BATTLED SUCCESSFULLY FOR THOLOCCO MILLIONS

WEWOKA, Mar. 1.—Grief that knows no color-line, and which is not confined to race, grips Seminole county today—Coody Johnson, Wewoka's first citizen, is dead. The distinguished freeman passed away in his palatial town mansion at 1:25 Saturday morning. The deceased had been on a decline physically for the past five years. His death was not unexpected. He was sixty-three years of age.

Perhaps no black man in Oklahoma has lived so colorful and hectic career as did Coody Johnson. From federal court interpreter for the five civilized tribes, during his early manhood, he was later drafted into the profession of law, having studied under the famous Federal Judge Parker of Ft. Smith, during the years when the old Indian Territory was in the making. He was an upstanding fighter for the rights of the Indians and freedman and finally ended his career as the dynamic force to snatch the millions from the estate of Barney Tholocco. In his declining years were marked with the touch of financial power that must have been in the hands of Midas.

Civil War Birth

J. Coody Johnson was born in 1864 in Seminole county, which at that time was just a portion of that vast domain known as the Creek Nation. He was the son of Robert and Elizabeth Johnson; the elder Johnson was in turn a member of the Okmulgee Council, interpreter for the Dawes Commission and an outstanding freedman who helped to shape the laws that barred the way of the outlaw and the grafters, and in fact form the underpinning of our present state constitution.

Early Schooling

Public schools were not in existence during the early years of young Coody's life, in the Indian Territory, but the Presbyterian church had established several missions where the rudiments of education were taught. It was in one of these lonely missions that the future financial giant learned of the three "R's" at the completion of his grammar school work at the mission, young Johnson was sent to Lincoln University, Chester, Penn., where he completed his college work.

Was Presbyterian

Early influences, during school life quite naturally caused Mr. Johnson to ally himself with the Presbyterian faith. He was a generous contributor to the mission work of this denomination, and practically all of his Christian activities were directed through this channel.

Coody Johnson
Crosses Divide

———

continued from page one

interpreter was finally transformed into a lawyer and admitted to practice in the federal court.

"Black Panther" Fame

After his admission to the bar, Coody Johnson moved to Wewoka. He began the practice of law, building up a wonderful practice. Perhaps the most important litigation in which he was engaged was the Barney Tholocco case. Tholocco was a destitute Indian who died, but whose allotment, shortly after his death developed one of the richest oil pools in the Southwest. Coody Johnson and his associates claimed to represent the rightful heir to this property. The case was long drawn out, extending over a period of nine years. Together with the men who joined in this historic battle, they organized the Black Panther Oil Company. The federal courts finally turned this vast fortune over to the Black Panther Oil Company. The property is worth millions.

Wife Comes to Rescue

It was while this Tholocco litigation was at fever heat that it almost seemed that the fates had turned an unkindly glance on Coody Johnson. Always a man of great and abiding faith in his efforts, he had staked his all on winning this court battle. He mortgaged his holdings in Seminole county, with which to raise funds to prolong the struggle. He married an Oklahoma City girl in 1910, and a young woman of much ability. This young woman who was Miss Anna Rolfe, prior to her marriage, and a teacher in the Oklahoma City schools, came into the financial breech. Just before the financial crises came, Mrs. Johnson had opened a ladies' ready-to wear. The venture was a success from the moment that the doors opened on the establishment. For several years it was the only gleam of hope, due to the business ability of Mrs. Johnson. The store grew to be the largest store of its kind in Wewoka. It, in fact, proved to be the rock upon which this couple stood until fortune again smiled upon them.

Valuable Holdings

Judge Johnson, as he was known in his latter years, had more than 1500 acres of land in Seminole county, in the vicinity of Wewoka; much of it is located near the territory that is being developed in that section of the state, and which is said to be the greatest oil pool in Oklahoma. In addition, he own two brick buildings in the city of Wewoka, three frame hotels and numerous rent houses. His monthly income in rentals in the city of Wewoka exceeded more than $2,000 per month so it is said. His home is one of the most modern and complete in this section.

Had Children

The deceased was married twice. By his first wife four children were born. Two now survive—Julius Johnson and Cressie Johnson, both of Wewoka. The funeral is being held in Wewoka today. Prominent Masons from all sections of Oklahoma are attending.

Was Grand Master

In early life Coody Johnson identified himself with the Masonic order; he helped in the first early struggles in the Indian Territory for Masonic life. He was rewarded for his services with elevation of Grand Master by St. John Grand Lodge, following the leadership of the late L. A. Bell.

Impressive eulogy. Dr. Whitby said that as a mason, the deceased was outstanding for his acts of charity.

Pall Bearers

The active pall bearers were; N. J. Caesar, Shawnee, J. T. Armstrong, Luther, Roscoe Dunjee, Oklahoma City, J. G. Floyd Wewoka, Robert Gay, Oklahoma City, and Dr. A. E. Beatty, Haskell.

The honorary pall bearers were: Dr. A. B. Whitby, Oklahoma City, A. G. W. Sango, Tulsa, W. H. Twine, Muskogee, S. E. Carson, Wewoka, Bennie Benjamin, Wewoka, Thomas Brunner, Seminole.

Buried Beside Father

The remains were interred in the family burial grounds, on one of the Johnson farms, one and one-half miles north of Wewoka.

Cards Among The Flowers

The following cards were found among the flowers:

St. John Grand Lodge, F. and A. M., Dr. A. Baxter Whitby; Officers and Directors of Exchange Trust Co., Tulsa; Indian friends, S. Willie Brown and Mrs. M. C. Jones, Wetumka; Colored Bar, Muskogee; Chamber of Commerce, Wewoka; Faculty and Students of Douglass High, Wewoka; Roscoe Dunjee, Oklahoma City; Mrs. L. Lena Sawner, Chandler, Unity Lodge, 106, F. and A. M., Wewoka; Sorosis Art and Literary Club, Wewoka; Mr. and Mrs. E. C. Aldridge, Wewoka; Mr. and Mrs. Thomas Edwards, Oklahoma City; Mrs. Alice Chatman, Wewoka; Miss Nannie Amey, Sapulpa; Miss Luella Lawson, Oklahoma City; Mr. and Mrs. P. W. Winslett, Oklahoma City; Mr. and Mrs. R. Benjamin, Wewoka; Mr. and Mrs. W. C. Bunyard, Wewoka; The community, Wewoka; Mr. and Mrs. Elmore Mitchell, Kansas City, Mo.; Mr. and Mrs. Fred Stumpp and Mr. and Mrs. Walter Stumpp, Wewoka; Thomas Electric Co., Wewoka; The

Mainards, Wewoka; Mr. and Mrs. E. R. Moore, Muskogee; W. H. Twine, Muskogee; Key Hardware Co., Wewoka; Mr. and Mrs. Jess McMullen, Wewoka; Wewoka Civic Club, Hershel Smith, Wewoka; Mr. and Mrs. A. M. Seran, Wewoka; Mr. and Mrs. E. C. Aldridge, Wewoka; Mr. and Mrs. B. F. Davis, Wewoka; St. John A. M. E. Sunday school, Wewoka; Rev. and Mrs. H. C. Cousins, Lima; Dr. D. C. Chandler, Holdenville; Miss Ware, Holdenville; Mrs. Cora Chiles, Holdenville; Mr. and Mrs. Granville Scales, Oklahoma City; Dr. and Mrs. E. B. Brooks, Oklahoma City; J. H. Lilly, Boley; Mrs. J. Chandler, and daughter, W. L. Thurston, Mrs. Alice B. Davis, Tom Holsey, and family, Dr. McDonald, Order of Eastern Star, Mrs. Viola Chandler, C. Guy Cutlipp and family, Mr. and Mrs. M. H. Perkins, Mr. and Mrs. T. S. Cobb, Mr. and Mrs. C. C. George, Mr. George Baker, Mrs. J. A. Baker, Mrs. J. A. Baker, Mrs. Lucy Baker, Mrs. Alice B. Davis.

Article II

I

Johnson Has Impressive Funeral

———

WEWOKA, Mar. 1.—Prominent Masons from all sections of Oklahoma gathered here today to perform the last sad rites over the deceased form of the late J. Coody Johnson. The funeral was held at the First Baptist church, and the services were in charge of the Rev. J. H. Hoard of Okmulgee.

The funeral party arrived at the church promptly at 1:30 and the services opened with singing "Take It To The Lord In Prayer." The church was filled with both white and colored citizens and the casket, a steel grey state couch, was covered with more than $500.00 worth of flowers.

"Other foundation can no man lay than Jesus the Christ" was the text taken by Rev. H. C. Cousins of Lima who preached the funeral sermon. The eloquent pulpiteer brought tears to the eyes of the audience as he told of the last fleeting moments of the deceased and the esteem in which he was held by his fellow-men in the community where he lived.

Mrs. J. E. Gorman sang "Face To Face" following which Rev. John M. Vie, white, pastor of the First Baptist church, Wewoka, eulogized the deceased.

White Pastor Talks

"I count it a distinct honor to have known Coody Johnson and to represent his many friends among my race here today", said Rev. Vie. "When I think of the character of the man, of his dogged tenacity, in the face of difficulty, discouragement; when I think of his strong mental capacity, I am willing to turn to the white as well as the colored people in this audience say that they too should strive to measure up to the splendid manhood of my friend who we shall bury today.

"He must have been a man of great courage, or he could not have overcome the many obstacles in his pathway. He built lasting friendships; today he is mourned by men and women of three races— the black man, the white man and the Indian. To think that he should spend his whole life in this community—born here, and yet through all the years never violate a trust, and in all the ways that men grow, was the greatest of them all.

He built lasting friendships; today he is mourned by men and women of three races—the black man, the white man and the Indian. To think that he should spend his whole life in this community—born here, and yet through all the years never violate a trust, and in all the ways that men grow, was the greatest of them all.

"The lesson that should come home to every colored boy and girl in this audience and in this community is this: Coody Johnson reached no heights, no eminence in the estimation of the white man, the Indian or among his own race, that is not possible of achievement for every black man."

"I repeat, I consider it an honor to have been his friends, and I express the wish, on behalf of the white people of this community, that you will give us again, out of your own race another character such as was J. Coody Johnson."

Resolutions

Following the reading of the obituary by Prof. J. G. Floyd and resolutions representing the A. M. E. church Douglass High school, Wewoka civic league, read by Prof. Wm. Frazier, the services were turned over to Grand Master A. Baxter Whitby, of St. John Grand Lodge who delivered a very impressive eulogy. Dr. Whitby said that as a mason, the deceased was outstanding for his acts of charity.

Pall Bearers

The active pall bearers were: N. J. Caesar, Shawnee, J. T. Armstrong. Luther, Roscoe Dunjee, Oklahoma City, J. G. Floyd Wewoka, Robert Gay, Oklahoma City, and Dr. A. E. Beatty, Haskell.

The honorary pall bearers were: Dr. A. B. Whitby, Oklahoma City, A. G. W. Sango, Tulsa, W. H. Twine, Muskogee, S. E. Carson, Wewoka, Bennie Benjamin, Wewoka, Thomas Brunner, Seminole.

Buried Beside Father

The remains were interred in the family burial grounds, on one of the Johnson farms, one and one-half miles north of Wewoka.

Cards Among The Flowers

The following cards were found among the flowers:

St. John Grand Lodge, F. and A. M., Dr. A. Baxter Whitby; Officers and Directors of Exchange Trust Co., Tulsa; Indian friends, S. Willie Brown and Mrs. M. C. Jones, Wetumka; Colored Bar, Muskogee; Chamber of Commerce, Wewoka; Faculty and Students of Douglass High, Wewoka; Roscoe Dunjee, Oklahoma City; Mrs. L. Lena Sawner, Chandler, Unity Lodge, 106, F. and A. M., Wewoka; Sorosis Art and Literary Club, Wewoka; Mr. and Mrs. E. C. Aldridge, Wewoka; Mr. and Mrs. Thomas Edwards, Oklahoma City; Mrs. Alice Chatman, Wewoka; Miss Nannie Amey, Sapulpa; Miss Luella Lawson, Oklahoma City; Mr. and Mrs. P. W. Winslett, Oklahoma City; Mr. and Mrs. R. Benjamin, Wewoka; Mr. and Mrs. W. C. Bunyard, Wewoka; The community, Oklahoma City; Mr. and Mrs. R. Benjamin, Wewoka; Mr. and Mrs. W. C. Bunyard, Wewoka; The community, Wewoka; Mr. and Mrs. Elmore Mitchell, Kansas City, Mo.; Mr. and Mrs. Fred Stumpp and Mr. and Mrs. Walter Stumpp, Wewoka; Thomas Electric Co., Wewoka; The Mainards, Wewoka; Mr. and Mrs. E. R. Moore, Muskogee; W. H. Twine, Muskogee; Key Hardware Co., Wewoka; Mr. and Mrs. Jess McMullen, Wewoka; Wewoka Civic Club,

Herahel Smith, Wewoka; Mr. and Mrs. A. M. Seran, Wewoka; Mr. and Mrs. E. C. Aldridge, Wewoka; Mr. and Mrs. B. F. Davis, Wewoka; St. John A.M.E. Sunday school, Wewoka; Rev. and Mrs. H. C. Cousins, Lima; Dr. D. C. Chandler, Holdenville; Miss Ware, Holdenville; Mrs. Cora Chiles, Holdenville; Mr. and Mrs. Granville Scales, Oklahoma City; Dr. and Mrs. E. B. Brooks, Oklahoma City; J. H. Lilly, Boley; Mrs. J. Chandler, and daughter, W. L. Thurston, Mrs. Alice B. Davis, Tom Holsey, and family, Dr. McDonald, Order of Eastern Star, Mrs. Viola Chandler, C. Guy Outlipp and family, Mr. and Mrs. M. H. Perkins, Mr. and Mrs. T. S. Cobb, Mr. and Mrs. C. C. George Mr. George Baker, Mrs. J. A. Baker, Mrs. J. A. Baker, Mrs. Lucy Baker, Mrs. Alice B. Davis.

Another Way

The passing of J. Coody Johnson this week removes from the scene of action and from life one of the most unique characters that has been produced from the fast fading group of Negroes who grew up under the influence of Indian customs and imbibed of Indian environment, and who we designate as freedmen.

Coody Johnson was born a slave. His father was one of those refugee black men who gathered around Fort Gibson during the Civil War period and later made his residence among the Five Civilized Tribes.

Possessed of an indomitable and courageous spirit, transmitted to him by his father, young Johnson grew up in the atmosphere of college environment that snatched him away from the baneful influences that seems to dominate and control blacks who lived in the Indian country. Later, his years as interpreter in the federal court that lifted him above the status of many whites, Indians and members of his own race, and his subsequent entrance into the profession of law, all tended to cloister him from the touch of an inferiority complex. Most of the men whom he contacted, of all races in the Indian Territory, and at Fort Smith, he met them as their superior. The kindly hands of fate manufactured out of Coody Johnson A MAN, although he was black, and although all about him and everywhere the spirit that makes slaves of men was being generated.

There are those among the Negro race who perhaps did not like J. Coody Johnson because of that freedom of view that could recognize no color line. Most Negroes do not know that they are just about as prejudiced towards whites as whites toward blacks. Not so with Coody; he could not think of business in the terms of NEGRO BUSINESS. He did not have a BLACK PERSPECTIVE; he saw men, not races, and so it was that J. Coody Johnson went out into the business world to measure arms with all men.

He formed business partnerships with white men or with black men or with Indians; the only equation with him to determine was the innate character of the man. How well he succeeded is history. It is an ancient belief among Negroes—most of them—that business partnerships with white men only mean that the Negro will be beaten out of his patrimony, and that he becomes the puppet of his white associate.

Inadvertently, the Negro who labors and suffers under the weight of such a psychology does not realize that he makes admission then of his inferior mental capacities. Coody Johnson was not afraid to stake his claim for millions with white associates. There is no record extant that proves that he was ever beaten out of a dollar. The record on the other hand, shows that through and by his great mental powers he was able to command respect of his associates, and that they loved him as a brother.

There are those who attended the funeral, who observing the numbers of whites present, are still wont to say, "They are here because they are after what he has." The writer got no such impression. Only a prejudiced mind could draw any such conclusions. In another column on this page we publish the utterances of a white minister of Wewoka. We hope our readers will turn and read it. There is a message of inter-racial good will. This is what we have been crying aloud for here in America, a chance to be understood.

Out of the life of Coody Johnson the white people of Wewoka understand black folk better. Those who know will tell you when the mob spirit was breaking in the little city several years ago, it was Coody who walked into the street to call white folk by their first name and shame them back to their door.

He saw men, not races, and so it was that J. Coody Johnson went out into the business world to measure arms with all men.

He formed business partnerships with white men or with black men or with Indians; the only equation with him to determine was the innate character of the man. How well he succeeded is history. It is an ancient belief among Negroes—most of them—that business partnerships with white men only mean that the Negro will be beaten out of his patrimony, and that he becomes the puppet of his white associate.

Inadvertently, the Negro who labors and suffers under the weight of such a psychology does not realize that he makes admission then of his inferior mental capacities. Coody Johnson was not afraid to stake his claim for millions with white associates. There is no record extant that proves that he was ever beaten out of a dollar. The record on the other hand, shows that through and by his great mental powers he was able to command respect of his associates, and that they loved him as a brother.

There are those who attended the funeral, who observing the numbers of whites present, are still wont to say, "They are here because they are after what he has." The writer got no such impression. Only a prejudiced mind could draw any such conclusions. In another column on this page we publish the utterances of a white minister of Wewoka. We hope our readers will turn and read it. There is a message of inter-racial good will. This is what we have been crying aloud for here in America, a chance to be understood.

Out of the life of Coody Johnson the white people of Wewoka understand black folk better. Those who know will tell you when the mob spirit was breaking in the little city several years ago, it was Coody who walked into the street to call white folk by their first name and shame them back to their door.

The Black Dispatch believes in Negro business, we believe in the opportunity that black business will give to the Negro boy and girl; but at the same time let us build symetrically and whole. When you find the opportunity to put money into white business, put it there also, and just as quickly as you would put it into a Negro business, when you have satisfied yourself that the project is sound and an economic necessity in your community.

There would have been no wholesale burning down of property in the city of Tulsa if the Negroes' homes had been mingled in and through the whites; and, it is quite likely that the whites who stopped the mob in Wewoka were Coody's business associates. J. Coody Johnson was worth more to them alive than he was dead.

"I can not hate a man I know," so said Charles Lamb. We wish some of our rich Negroes here in Oklahoma could purchase stock in the American National Bank of Oklahoma City, or in the Exchange National Bank of Tulsa. The ice must be broken; we can not forever remain wholly detached in an economic way from the white man here in America and expect to solve our economic problems. Dollars rule the world and Negroes must find a place on the directorate that controls American dollars. Coody Johnson pointed the way to an economic understanding between white and black dollars, and he also proved that out of such contact there developed a brotherhood unbroken by the grave.

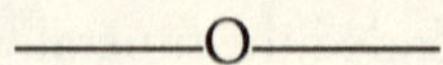

Research Report Assignment References

1. Black Dispatch Newspaper—1919-1927
2. Seminole Indian Nation—Wewoka, Oklahoma
3. Zellar, Gary, African Creeks: Estelvste and the Creek Nation (Norman: University of Oklahoma Press, 1927).
4. Oral History—Johnson Grove Alumni (Browns—Henry and Ruddy) (Hunts) (Kemps)
5. Hawkins Steve Oklahoma Historical Society

   琀

   www.OklahomaHistoricalLibrary.com
6. Taulbert, P. Oklahoma Library,

   琀

   www.OklahomaResearchLibrary.com

www.ingramcontent.com/pod-product-compliance
Lightning Source LLC
Chambersburg PA
CBHW022042050726
47591CB00003B/919